W9-AES-545

AMERICAN LEGENDS™

Molly Pitcher

Frances E. Ruffin

TOWNSHIP OF UNION
FREE PUBLIC LIBRARY

The Rosen Publishing Group's
PowerKids Press™
New York

For Elizabeth McCombs, a librarian who devoted a lifetime to bringing together children and books

Published in 2002 by The Rosen Publishing Group, Inc.
29 East 21st Street, New York, NY 10010

First Edition

Book Design: Michael de Guzman
Project Editor: Kathy Campbell

Photo Credits: p. 4 © CORBIS-BETTMANN; p. 7 © Index Stock; p. 8 © Stock Montage; p. 11 © Bridgeman Art Library; p. 12 © North Wind Pictures; p. 15 © North Wind Pictures; p. 16 © Archive Photos; p. 19 © Bettmann/CORBIS; p. 20 © North Wind Pictures.

Ruffin, Frances E.
Molly Pitcher / Frances E. Ruffin.— 1st ed.
    p. cm. — (American legends)
Includes index.
ISBN 0-8239-5829-9 (library binding)
1. Pitcher, Molly, 1754–1832—Juvenile literature. 2. Monmouth, Battle of, 1778—Juvenile literature. 3. Revolutionaries—United States—Biography—Juvenile literature. 4. United States—History—Revolution, 1775–1783—Biography—Juvenile literature.
[1. Pitcher, Molly, 1754-1832. 2. United States—History—Colonial period, ca. 1600–1775. 3. United States—History—Revolution, 1775–1783.
4. Women—Biography.] I. Title. II. Series.
E241.M7 P576 2002
973.3'34'092—dc21

00-012484

$13.95

I B
PITCHER MOLLY
c.1

Manufactured in the United States of America

Contents

Few women have ever been so at home on a battlefield as had Molly Pitcher. Today the U.S. Army presents The Honorable Order of Molly Pitcher award to deserving male and female soldiers.

Molly Pitcher

This is a story about the brave American **patriot** Molly Pitcher. Some people believe that Molly never existed or that parts of her story have been made up. Others believe that she really did live and that her name was Mary Ludwig.

As a young girl, Molly had many adventures. Some of them might have helped her later to become a famous heroine in America's **Revolutionary War** (1775–83). During America's war for freedom from Great Britain, she followed her soldier husband into battle. When her injured husband fell beside his cannon at the Battle of Monmouth, she took his place and fired away until the end of the battle. Her actions made Molly a **legend**.

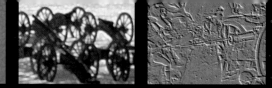

What Is a Legend?

Some stories are told over and over again, often because the people are **heroic**, and the events are exciting. With each telling of a story, the special qualities about someone, or the real facts about events, become **exaggerated**. A good example of this is how Molly became known as Molly Pitcher. Some people say she was first called Molly Pitcher as a child, when she served water to troops who passed her family's farm. Others say she earned her name as an adult when she brought pitchers of water to soldiers during an important battle in the American Revolution. However she got her name, Mary Ludwig, known as Molly Pitcher, was a true American patriot.

We learn about people who lived long ago and about events that happened in the past from stories called legends.

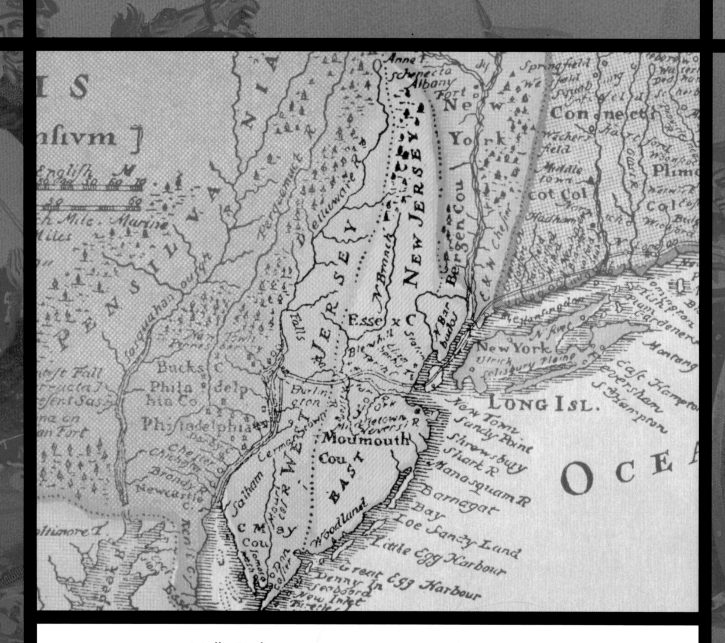

Molly Pitcher grew up near Trenton, New Jersey,
where her family owned a dairy farm.

A Farm in Trenton

There are no records of Mary Ludwig's birth, but most historians believe she was born on October 13, 1754. Everyone called her Molly, including her two older brothers, Joshua and Joseph, and her younger brother, Carl.

Molly's parents, John and Gretchen Ludwig, owned a dairy farm near Trenton, New Jersey. Like many **colonists**, Molly's parents had **emigrated** from Europe to seek a better life in America. John Ludwig had come from Germany and Gretchen had come from Holland. They had moved to the American **colonies** before Molly was born. Most of the families around Trenton were also settlers who owned farms.

Colonists and Native Americans

At one time, the land on which the Ludwig farm stood was forest. During the early 1700s, more and more colonists moved into lands that had belonged to Native Americans. Several wars were fought between British soldiers, who helped the colonists, and Native American warriors. Molly's brother Joseph joined the soldiers. There was peace in New Jersey and in the eastern part of its neighboring colony, Pennsylvania. A **treaty** was offered to keep the peace between the colonists and Native Americans. Most of the Native Americans had moved west, beyond the mountains that divided the eastern and western areas of Pennsylvania.

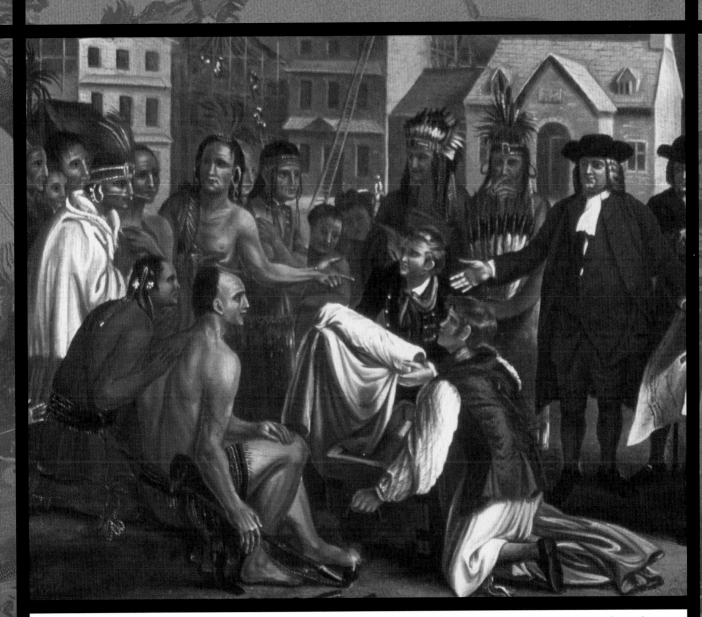

The Native Americans were unhappy about the colonists taking their lands.
For many years there was a struggle between the two groups over the land,
including the area of New Jersey where Molly's family lived.

Molly was a hard worker. She helped with chores done around
her parents' farm, including milking the cows.

A Colonial Childhood

Molly had a happy and busy childhood. Like most children who grew up on a farm in the colonies, Molly had many **responsibilities**. From an early age, she helped her mother keep their house clean. She also had to do **chores** around the farm. She milked cows, fed chickens, and helped plant vegetables in the family garden. Her father sold the milk, butter, and cheese made from their cows. Molly got help from her younger brother, Carl, when he wasn't in school. Few girls were sent to school during colonial times. At that time, people felt that it would be a waste to teach girls to read and write and do math. Molly, however, wished that she, too, could be taught to read and write.

Taxes and Troops

During the spring of 1765, Molly's family learned that they would have to pay a tax on some of the things they needed in their everyday lives. This was a **hardship** for the Ludwigs and other Americans. Around that time, troops of colonial soldiers began to pass the Ludwigs' farmhouse. These soldiers were going to meet British soldiers in western Pennsylvania. They wanted to make sure that the peace treaty between the colonists and Native Americans would be kept. Molly greeted the tired soldiers with a bucket of cool water. According to legend, whenever she missed soldiers who waited for the water, they called out, "Molly! Molly, pitcher!" to get her attention.

A tax on tea, sugar, and other items was ordered by King George III of England to help pay the expenses of the wars that were fought with Native Americans in the colonies.

British taxes made it difficult for Molly's family to earn a living. Molly was invited to work in the home of family friends from Carlisle, Pennsylvania. For her services, Dr. Irvine and his wife offered to pay the Ludwigs one year's worth of taxes.

A Dangerous Trip

Molly helped her parents by working for family friends, Dr. and Mrs. Irvine. She went with them to Carlisle, Pennsylvania, where they lived. When they tried to cross the Delaware River, storm winds forced the barge on which their wagon was loaded into some rocks. Quick-thinking Molly cut the wagon's cloth cover with the doctor's knife. This action stopped the boat from sinking. Farther on, they spent the night at an inn where Molly and Mrs. Irvine overheard the innkeeper's plans to steal their horses and wagon, which was full of goods. It sounded like the innkeeper might even try to harm them. Bravely, they crept past the sleeping innkeeper, warned Dr. Irvine, and quietly left with all of their possessions.

Molly at Valley Forge

Molly worked for the Irvines for several years. By 1775, Molly was 21 years old and was married to John Casper Hays. American colonists no longer wanted to pay the king's taxes. They wanted to become an independent nation with their own laws. It wasn't long before war broke out. After her husband joined the **Continental army**, Molly felt that it was also her duty to help the soldiers. During the very cold winter of 1777–78, Molly was one of several wives who traveled to the battlefield at Valley Forge, Pennsylvania. These women joined Martha Washington in carrying food, bandages, extra clothes, and blankets for their husbands. Months later, the fighting moved closer to Molly's home.

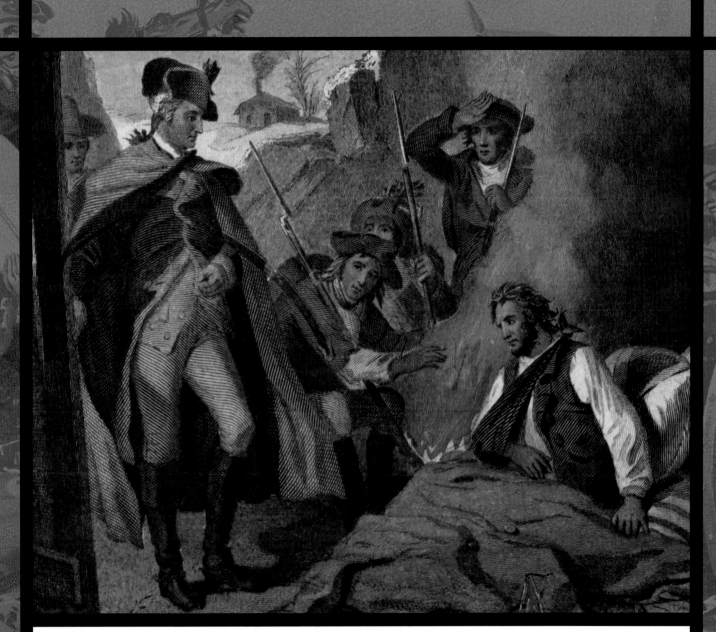

In 1775, colonial patriots formed the Continental army, and George Washington (seen here at Valley Forge) was its commander in chief. This new army was created to fight King George III's army.

When Molly saw her husband injured and lying by his cannon, she quickly gave him a drink of water and grabbed the cannon's rammer, loaded it, and shot. She continued to shoot until evening!

Molly and Her Pitcher Go to War

On June 28, 1778, it was a fiercely hot day. The Continental and British armies were camped in Monmouth County, New Jersey. This was only several miles (km) from the Ludwig farm. Molly was worried that the heat would be dangerous, and that the American soldiers would need water during battle. Taking a large pitcher, she rode her horse to the battlefield. Through the cannon fire, Molly saw that the men were tired and very thirsty. She ran to a nearby spring and repeatedly filled her pitcher to carry the water to the soldiers. Some men who knew her called out, "Molly, pitcher!" Other men, thinking that this was her name, also called, "Here, Molly Pitcher!"

Sergeant Molly

Hearing of her bravery, General George Washington named her a "**sergeant**" in the Continental army. She also was awarded an army **pension** of $40 every year for the rest of her life.

After the war, Molly and John Hays had a quiet life until John died, around 1789. Molly later married a man named George McCauley. She had never had children. Mary Ludwig Hays McCauley, known as Molly Pitcher, died on January 22, 1832, at the age of 78. She was buried in Carlisle, Pennsylvania, with military honors.

Glossary

chores (CHORZ) The tasks or jobs that a person performs daily.

colonies (KAH-luh-neez) Areas in a new country where a large group of people move, who are still ruled by the leaders of their old country.

colonists (KAH-luh-nists) People who live in a colony.

Continental army (kon-tin-EN-tul AR-mee) The army of patriots created in 1775, with George Washington as its commander in chief.

emigrated (EH-mih-gray-ted) Having left one country to settle in another.

exaggerated (ihg-ZAH-juh-ray-ted) Having made something to seem larger or more amazing than it really is.

hardship (HARD-ship) An event that causes great difficulty or pain.

heroic (hih-ROH-ik) To be brave and noble.

legend (LEJ-end) A story passed down through the years that many people believe.

patriot (PAY-tree-ot) A person who loves and defends his or her country.

pension (PEN-shun) A specific amount of money paid when a person retires from a job or from the military.

responsibilities (rih-spon-sih-BIH-lih-teez) Things that a person must take care of or complete.

Revolutionary War (reh-vuh-LOO-shuh-nayr-ee WOR) The war that American colonists fought from 1775 to 1783 to win independence from England.

sergeant (SAR-jint) An army or a marine officer.

treaty (TREE-tee) A formal agreement that is signed by at least two nations.

Index

B
Battle of Monmouth, 5
British, 10, 14, 21

C
Carlisle, Pennsylvania, 17, 22
colonists, 9, 10, 14, 18
Continental army, 18, 22

G
Great Britain, 5

H
Hays, John Casper, 18, 22

L
Ludwig, Mary, 5

M
McCauley, George, 22
Monmouth County, New Jersey, 21

N
Native Americans, 10, 14

R
Revolutionary War, 5

T
Trenton, New Jersey, 9

V
Valley Forge, Pennsylvania, 18

W
Washington, George, 22
Washington, Martha, 18
water, 6, 14, 21

Web Sites

To learn more about Molly Pitcher, check out these Web sites:
http://sill-www.army.mil/pao/pamolly.htm
www.hobart.k12.in.us/gemedia/amrev/revbio/mpitcher.htm